THE ZAMPA LAW

THE ZAMPA LAW

Protecting Unaccompanied Migrant Minors in Italy

Elizabeth Bose O. Bien-Aime

MYSTERY PUBLISHERS
Redefining African Stories

The Zampa Law
Protecting Unaccompanied Migrant Minors in Italy

The information provided in this book is for informational purposes only. It is not intended to be a source of legal advice. The opinions expressed within this book are solely the author's and do not reflect the opinions and beliefs of the Government of the Republic of Italy.

Unless otherwise indicated, names used are fictitious. Although the publisher and the author have made every effort to ensure that the information in this book was correct, and while this publication is designed to provide accurate information regarding the subject matter covered, the publisher and the author assume no responsibility for errors, inaccuracies, omissions, or any other inconsistencies herein and hereby disclaim any liability to any party for any loss, damage, or disruption caused by errors or omissions, whether such errors or omissions result from negligence, accident, or any other cause.

A CIP record of this book is available from the Kenya National Library.

Kindle Edition, by Mystery Books, an imprint of Mystery Publishers - 2023

Paperback Edition

Published by:
Mystery Publishers Limited
P O BOX 18016 - 20100
Tel: +254 718 429 184
Nakuru, Kenya
Email: publishing@mysterypublisherslimited.com
www.mysterypublisherslimited.com

Cover design by Vincent de Paul ©Mystery Books
Typeset in Book Antiqua size 11 by Mystery Publishers Limited, Kenya
Design & Layout by Vincent de Paul ©Mystery Publishers Limited

Dedicated to

All Unaccompanied Migrant Minors

"

Remember that God puts us in a situation where we don't see a solution. We are forced to trust Him and not our ability, power, wisdom, etc.

If, by chance, you re-enter your passport country or reunite with your loved ones, it may not feel the way you have anticipated. Hence, embrace love and gratitude and impact positively in your host country.

"

Elizabeth Bose O. Bien-Aime

We owe our children—the most vulnerable citizens in any society—a life free from violence and fear.

Nelson Mandela

CONTENTS

LIST OF TABLES

PREFACE

THE NUMBER OF unaccompanied migrant minors in Italy has increased significantly in recent years. In turn, it has put a great burden on the Italian government regarding the protection and availability of legal guardians to those minors. Recently, the Italian Parliament passed Law 47/2017--the so-called Zampa Law following lobbying efforts and the release of UNICEF's 'Child Alert: A Deadly Journey for Children'. This landmark law was adopted on April 7, 2017, and attempts to organise the overlapping legislative provisions introduced in recent years. For the first time, The Zampa Law intends to create an organised legal system focusing on the protection and reception system for unaccompanied minors and children separated from their parents or guardians in Italy.

This book aims to contribute to a better understanding of the gap that the new Italian Zampa Law filled, as well as the challenges in applying the new law and other aspects of the Italian immigration system related to unaccompanied migrant minors. The Zampa Law has taken a bold step to measure up to international standards on the protection of unaccompanied migrant minors in Italy despite some challenges. The fact remains that the new Law is still in its infancy stage; hence, to promote effectiveness in guardianship, it would require a joint effort of all stakeholders in translating it from the theoretical level to practical implementation.

All stakeholders have agreed upon this to prolong the UN Sustainable Development Goals (SDGs) Agenda 2030.

ACKNOWLEDGEMENTS

MY HIGHEST GRATITUDE goes to God Almighty for His grace that enabled me to sail through my study in Rome, Italy.

I sincerely appreciate my husband, Rico Bien-Aime, for his financial support; thank you, Ms Sandra Baffoe-Bonnie, Ms Chigozirim Bodart, Ms Kankemwa Zakariya, Mr Desire Yetsowiu Assogbavi, Victoria Yvonne-Bien-Aime, and Ms Caroline Baaro whose generosity has afforded me this opportunity.

Thank you: to the staff of Prolaw Loyola University Chicago (John Felice Rome Center) and everyone whose generosity afforded me this unique opportunity; my supervisor Professor Anna Koppel, who wisely guided my research; Professor Bill Loris; Professor Karen Shaw, for your razor-sharp intellect, motivation and inspiration; Professor Karen Shaw for your commitment and insight; Professor Thomas McInerney, for being considerate during the time of difficulties; Ms Helena Lundgren-Doyle for your calm deposition in tackling my various concerns; Ms Vanessa Cariso for your willingness to listen and act promptly; and Ms Ann for being such a great help when navigating PROLAW John Felix Rome Centre Resources.

Special thanks to the Loyola University Chicago and the Loyola University Chicago School of Law for admitting me to the LLM in the Rule of Law for Development program and for selecting me for the Rule of Law Scholarship and Fellowship award, PROLAW Rome award and other awards. I am thankful to the experienced professors and practitioners for their vast contributions to my personal and professional growth in practice.

Thank you: Sebastiano Cannizzo for giving my colleague and me free accommodation during my research in Sicily and your good friend Richard Bordie for your help on migration; Calleri, Mariarosy, and Daniel for your encouragement on Video media; and Francesca Bruzzese for your Italian lessons.

To my Fellow leaders of Prolaw 7 of the 2017/2018 Programme, thank you for the amazing memories, and my good friend, Adebayo Francis Alowolodu—I have found a great friend in you.

Finally, I appreciate my publisher, Vincent de Paul, for his professional guidance during the publishing process and the rest of the Mystery Publishers team for their invaluable input into the book.

INTRODUCTION

WE LIVE IN a world faced with a plethora of turmoil, from conflicts, civil war, and other calamities, causing people to flee for their lives. This is most evident in places like Syria, Libya, Palestine, and many sub-Saharan African countries, where people have been left homeless and live in venerable and desperate conditions that require them to seek a safe haven for survival.

The most vulnerable are migrant minors who are separated from their immediate family members during these perilous journeys. These minors are susceptible to danger as they are defenceless and are at risk of child trafficking. In addition, these fleeing children are faced with immigration restrictions at the border of every country they run to, from not being allowed to enter to being sent back by the authorities even after succeeding in moving into the country.

In this scenario, the Zampa Law for 'Provision of Protection Measures' is meant to amend the immigration and tools on the status of foreign children (legislative decree 25 July 1998 No. 286). This law is a boon to the children fleeing for their lives without being accompanied by any family member or guardian in Italy.

ABBREVIATIONS

AIDA Asylum International Database

ASGI Association for Juridical Studies on Immigration

CSOs Civil Society Organisations

ECRE European Council Refugees and Exiles

EMN European Migration Network

GDI General Dependent for Immigration

IC RMW International Convention on the Protection of the Rights of All Migrant Workers and Members of their Families

INCPS Italy National Child Protection Systems

IOM International Organization for Migration

NGOs Non-Governmental Organizations

SDGs UN Sustainable Development Goals

SPRAR Protection System for Refugee and Asylum Seekers

SSN National Healthcare Service

UDHR Universal Declaration of Human Rights

UMM Unaccompanied Migrant Minors

UN United Nations

UNCRC United Nations Convention on the Rights of the Child

UNECA United Nations Economic Commission for Africa

UNESCO United Nations Educational, Scientific and Cultural Organisation

UNHCR United Nations High Commissioner for Refugees

UNICEF United Nations International Children's Emergency Fund

UNPF United Nations Population Fund

The Zampa Law

CHAPTER ONE

The Unaccompanied Minor

IT WAS A COLD MORNING in October, just before the sun rose when Maria (not her real name) was handed over by her father to a smuggler on a fishing boat. Maria was only four years old. The fishing boat was headed from her home country to the safer shores of the Italian island of Lampedusa. Her father was a man on a mission, trying to save his family. He had walked much faster than his wife and seven-year-old son, and when he reached the boat, he had decided to hand over the toddler and go back for the others. With a hasty goodbye, Maria's father left her alongside strangers in the makeshift boat, unaware of what was happening around her. However, before her family could make their way back, the boat left, and she was on her own.

Many of her fellow citizens have secretly journeyed from the coastal town. However, the clandestine 80-mile trip to the Italian Island has often been intercepted, and those making the journey would be sent back to their country of origin. Still, Maria, unaccompanied by her parents or a legal guardian, and the others managed to get to Italy despite battling tough conditions aboard the makeshift boat. Maria ended up in the hands of authorities, who, after deliberation, decided that the best action plan was to return her to the land she had fled from. Back home, Maria's parents were detained for attempting to flee and endangering their children's lives but were later released. In the end, Maria was reunited with her family.

FACTS AND FIGURES

Maria's case is not an isolated event. There are over 21.3 million people seeking refuge in various countries worldwide. More than half of these migrants are unaccompanied minors forced to survive in various refugee camps. These are citizens of a developing country under eighteen years old and regarded as stateless persons on arrival in the territory of a neighbouring country without being escorted by a grown-up person responsible for their well-being, legally or by tradition. In 2016, there were about 26,000 unaccompanied minors that came to the shores of southern Italy.[1] Furthermore, the number of unaccompanied children registered in April 2017 was 16,000, while 5,000 were recorded missing. Some of

[1] (United Nations n.d.)

these missing cases were because some tried to link up with their family members spread across Europe and/or to find a better way of life.[2]

Equally, the Dublin III Regulation of 2017 and the Relocation Scheme of 2015 have legally given recognition to unaccompanied children to move from Italy to other European countries. In recent years, however, many of these unaccompanied migrant minors have been deported back to Italy by some of the neighbouring European countries like France, Austria, and Switzerland. There are reports of about 600 unaccompanied migrant minors deported to Italy by the Switzerland authorities in 2016, and these children are forced to stay in Italy against their desires.[3]

Over the years, Italy has become a major entry point for refugees, asylum seekers and, among them, unaccompanied migrant minors coming from the Middle East and Africa due to the comparatively close proximity of its southern coast to the northern coastline of North Africa relative to other European borders. The Italian government has put great effort and resources into rescuing, sheltering and feeding the migrants and unaccompanied minors on their arrival. However, it has been noted and reported that the Reception Centres have deprived [the unaccompanied minors] of their liberty without a statutory basis, formal detention order, or a judicial review, in breach of international obligations, the Italian Constitution

2 (Office Of Refugee Resettlement 2019)

3 (UNICEF 2019)

and national legislation forbidding the[ir] detention … in centres for identification and expulsion.

According to a recent report on the situation of unaccompanied minors in Italy[4], '*the war and refugee flow from Ukraine led to a sharp increase in the number of unaccompanied minors arriving in Italy, which nearly doubled in comparison with the previous year. As of 30 June 2022, there are 15 595 unaccompanied minors in Italy (an increase of 99.9%). The report shows that these unaccompanied minors are mostly male (80.1%) and mostly 17 years old (44.8%). They arrived primarily from Ukraine (5,932), Egypt (2,497), Albania (1,302), Bangladesh (1,239) and Tunisia (1,145). The increase in minors fleeing Ukraine influenced the age and gender distribution of the group overall in comparison with previous years where there has been a decrease in the percentage of those aged 17 and an increase in that of those aged 15, as well as an increase in the number of girls.*'

Definition of Unaccompanied Minors

United Nations Committee on the Rights of the Child (UNCRC) defines Unaccompanied minors and children as those *who have been separated from both parents and other relatives and are not being cared for by an adult who, by law or custom, is responsible for doing so* and separated children, those who have been separated from both parents, or from their previous legal or

4 (Ministry of Labor and Social Policies - Directorate for Immigration and Integration Policies 2020)

customary primary caregiver, but not necessarily from other relatives.

Similarly, according to the United Nations High Commissioner for Refugees (UNHCR)—the Refugee Convention of 1951—*'Unaccompanied children' (also referred to as unaccompanied minors) are children, as defined in article 1 of the Convention, who have been separated from both parents and other relatives and are not being cared for by an adult, who by the law of custom, is responsible for doing so'.*

Protection of Unaccompanied Minors

The resolution adopted by the Human Rights Council on 28 September 2017 at the 39th UN General Assembly Meeting[5] is fundamental to protecting these unaccompanied minors. The resolution has thirteen articles and urges States parties to consider the child's best interests by safeguarding the unaccompanied children from violence, exploitation, and abuse. The resolution encourages states to promote and protect the fundamental human rights of migrants, irrespective of their status, with equal protection to unaccompanied minors within their territories. The member states are also urged to consider in their immigration policies the integration of the child's best interest concerning unaccompanied children crossing borders.

5 (UN General Assembly 2017)

Motivators to Migrate

Many reasons cause people to flee their countries, including:

- persons leaving their home countries when there is war and conflict. In such a situation, people will pack up a few belongings and leave using whatever means possible, whether by train, road or makeshift boats. In many situations where citizens flee from war, women and children will be the first to be considered to cross borders as they are considered to be more vulnerable;

- due to the effects of climate change, such as floods that have displaced them from their homes. Climate change has also resulted in reduced rainfall in some areas, causing drought and famine, incentivising people to leave their homes rather than risk starvation and death;

- the search for better jobs, education systems, and healthcare;

- in search of freedom from discrimination when they belong to a minority such as a tribe, gender identity, religious group or even a dissenting political ideology; and

- in most cases, parents move their families to new countries to ensure that their children get a better quality of life than what they would get by staying in their home countries. This ideology can help explain why so many children crossing the borders every year are at risk of becoming separated from their caregivers.

Why Children Become Separated From Their Parents

Many children become separated from their parents and caregivers because of varying factors. One cause of minors left without caregivers is death. Many caregivers will sacrifice themselves for their children, who end up suffering from malnutrition and ill health. Something as simple as ensuring that one's children have the only blanket available predisposes adults to extreme temperatures that may harm them. This instinctual drive puts parents and caregivers at risk, sometimes resulting in them not getting to shore with the minors.

Another reason minors become unaccompanied is that parents may not have the right documentation. This may cause parents to be detained by the authorities and get repatriated back to their country of origin. In other cases, parents will send their children away in the care of others because they might find greater sympathy and be let into the countries they are fleeing for simply being minors. In such cases, the children will be entrusted to smugglers who promise to sneak them past the border checks and deliver them to better lives abroad.

According to the laws in the many countries where the children are smuggled, there is legislation that supports and grants asylum to unaccompanied minors while their parents would not be treated in the same way. This gives rise to the situation where parents sacrifice to let their children travel alone. Unaccompanied minors may also be older teens running away from their home countries to join other family members already residing in another country. The child may have been separated from their family a long time ago and may not even be able to communicate that they are coming and therefore have other arrangements made to receive them. Thus, they may get lost while pursuing their relatives. These older children may also be seeking employment in the countries they fled to because of high poverty levels in their home countries.

Dangers Faced by Unaccompanied Minors

The journey to a foreign country, especially across waterways, is perilous. Aboard the boats, the children face abuse from the smugglers and traffickers responsible for getting them safely across to Italy. Minors are also likely to be used as drug mules to make them pay for the money they owe for the transport to the new land. The children will likely suffer from nutritional deficiencies, scabies, and other infectious diseases. The infectious diseases spread fast from one person to another due to lowered immunity, unhygienic conditions, and living in cramped quarters that often have poor ventilation. The survivors who reach the shores of Italy are often weak and dehydrated, needing assistance just to take steps off the boats. The strong winds and waves often bow boats off course, making the journeys much longer and more dangerous. Many people who set off do not make it to shore. Some people get lost, never to be found, while others perish when boats capsize.

On a psychological level, unaccompanied minors are likely to suffer separation anxiety and depression. The minors may display symptoms of stress, such as irritability, disrupted sleep, and decreased appetite. The trauma of separation is hard on minors, who may not adapt well to a transitional life in a new country. Even in relatively safe conditions, the child is likely to be unsettled and display characteristics of a person who has experienced abandonment. They may be clingy or the exact opposite, unable to form healthy attachments to others.

The abandoned child may hold onto an item from their previous life, such as a blanket or their parent's necklace or scarf. This is a method of coping with the anxieties surrounding the sudden change in their circumstances. The child may react violently or be extremely distressed should the item be taken away from them.

The long-term effects of this kind of traumatic event include poor health and academic outcomes, lower job prospects, and difficulty forming long-lasting relationships. These effects are due to a long-lasting distrust of the world because the child's feeling of safety is destroyed when they are separated from their parents.

Migrant Minors

To understand the full scope of the plight of unaccompanied minors, it is important to understand the broader concept of migrants. A migrant is defined by the UN International Organisation for Migration (IOM) as 'a person who permanently or temporarily lives in a country where he or she was not born or naturalised and has acquired some significant social ties to that country'[6].

Similarly, a migrant worker is defined by the International Convention on the Protection of the Rights of All Migrant workers and Members of Their Families (ICRMW) 1990 as '[a] person who is to be engaged, or has been engaged in a remunerated activity in a state of which he or she is not a national'.[7] Furthermore, according to Gabriela Rodríguez Pizarro, the first UN Special Rapporteur on the human rights of migrants,

6 (International Organisation for Migration (IOM) n.d.)
7 (International Convention on the Protection of the Rights of All Migrant Workers and Members of Their Families 1990)

a migrant can be a person who is firstly outside the territory of the states of which they are a citizen or national and is not subject to its national legal protection and is in the territory of another state(s)[8]. Secondly, the person does not enjoy the general legal protection of their fundamental rights by diplomatic agreements, visas, other agreements or the general legal recognition of rights which is inherent in the granting by the host states of the status of refugee, naturalised person, or similar status.

The child's main purpose for leaving their country may be for economic reasons or fleeing war. However, the child's right to employment was not considered in the United Nations Convention, but the Convention does urge the Member States to establish regulations on a minimum age for employment and the child working conditions, as well as measures to enforce sanctions to prevent the child's economic exploitation.

There is a need to stress the importance of a guardian as it relates to unaccompanied children. The Asylum Information Database (AIDA) states: A guardian is appointed when children do not have the legal capacity and no parents or other relatives or persons who could exercise parental authority are present in the territory. The guardian is responsible for the protection and well-being of the child. The procedure under Italian law for the appointment of a guardian is that they must be nominated within forty-eight hours.

8 (UN General Assembly 2017)

These children often find it challenging to make an appeal without having a guardian.

It is important to emphasise the numerous roles of a legal guardian in assisting unaccompanied minors coming into Italy. These include; escorting them for appointments at the immigration office, appearing with the minors at the interview centres, and helping them to process their asylum claims. Where a minor cannot get a legal guardian, they may be prone to abuse, neglect, exploitation, and unnecessary delayed procedures in the process of their claims.

Studies have shown that the Italian Reception Centres have received many unaccompanied migrant minors over the years. Many of them came from the world's less developed countries to arrive in Italy through perilous journeys, and once they arrived, they were left alone to survive. They lack access to clothing, food, protection, shelter, and baths.[9]

Furthermore, there were reports of human rights violations, particularly children's rights. Natalia Alonso also laments thus:

> The appalling experience of children in Italy is a harsh indicator of the failure of European governments and the Italian authorities to protect children coming in search of safety and dignity. It also exposes once again the failure of Europe's wider policy approach to place

9 (Reliefweb 2018)rt/italy/italy-more-100-unaccompanied-foreign-minors-helped-first-quarter-i-careabout-you

> the responsibilities of managing a common border upon only a few European countries. Europe must stand together to welcome the people arriving here, who are fleeing from conflict, persecution and other unbearable situations.[10]

The above comments are compounded by the fact that most of the unaccompanied migrant minors moving to Italy are ignorant and uninformed of their rights to make necessary requests for asylum claims not until after many months before they are aware of the required steps. Additionally, unaccompanied migrant minors are always facing unnecessary bureaucratic delays from officers of the Reception Centers and the local Immigration Service and Juvenile Tribunals. More so, some lucky unaccompanied children who can get to the Reception Center often face unnecessary delays for several months at the immigration service for appointments to process their identifications and temporary residence permits. The concerned authorities have associated the delays with a shortage of immigration officers at the Prefecture and Questura (provincial police headquarters), and the Juvenile Courts.

For some of the unaccompanied children who are lucky to have a guardian, their guardians would have

10 (Alonso, N. 2016. Europe is failing refugee and migrant children, Oxfam. Available online at https://www.oxfamamerica.org/press/europe-is-failing-refugee-and-migrant-children/. Accessed on 13/02/2018. n.d.)

to visit the office of immigration at Questura several times before being able to obtain asylum requests, residence permits, and identification on their behalf. Among the many challenges confronted by unaccompanied children seeking asylum are their accessibilities to legal guardians and representatives and the difficulties in getting residence permits.

CHAPTER TWO

International framework on Protection of Unaccompanied Migrant Minors

At one-and-a-half years old, Thomas (not his real name) found himself on a boat in the middle of a standoff. The boat was a non-government rescue boat that had just rescued him alongside 191 other unaccompanied minors. The minors were in the presence of adults, some of whom were sick and vulnerable.

Thomas was one of the lucky people to get off the boat and gain entrance into the coastal country of Italy through one of its ports alongside the other minors and the sick. They were quickly evaluated and attended to because they were hungry and unwell. They needed warmth and a safe place to stay. At that tender age, Thomas had witnessed a scene he would likely never remember.

While the minors were whisked off to safety, 35 adults remained on the boat. They were denied permission to enter the Italian borders. They were deemed healthy and not in dire need of rescue. The authorities at the port were given clear guidelines on who should and shouldn't be allowed to disembark.

The government further issued for the 35 adults to be taken in by the flag country to which the non-governmental organisation belonged. However, that boat and several others were denied entry into the country. Those against the move cited laws that required Italy to take on everyone who came calling on them. They opposed parties that challenged the government to allow the migrants safe passage into the rest of the landlocked countries. However, the government was adamant in its stance. They insisted that they would only guarantee entry and/or safe passage to minors and those who are sick and can otherwise not make the journey to another coastal port.

This is just one example of the complex humanitarian crisis when laws clash. However, the need to protect unaccompanied minors is universal. There exists a provision of legal protection for unaccompanied migrant minors laid down in different legal instruments. The fundamental legal framework for unaccompanied migrant minors is further illustrated below:

Chart 1: International Legal Instrument for Unaccompanied Migrant Minors

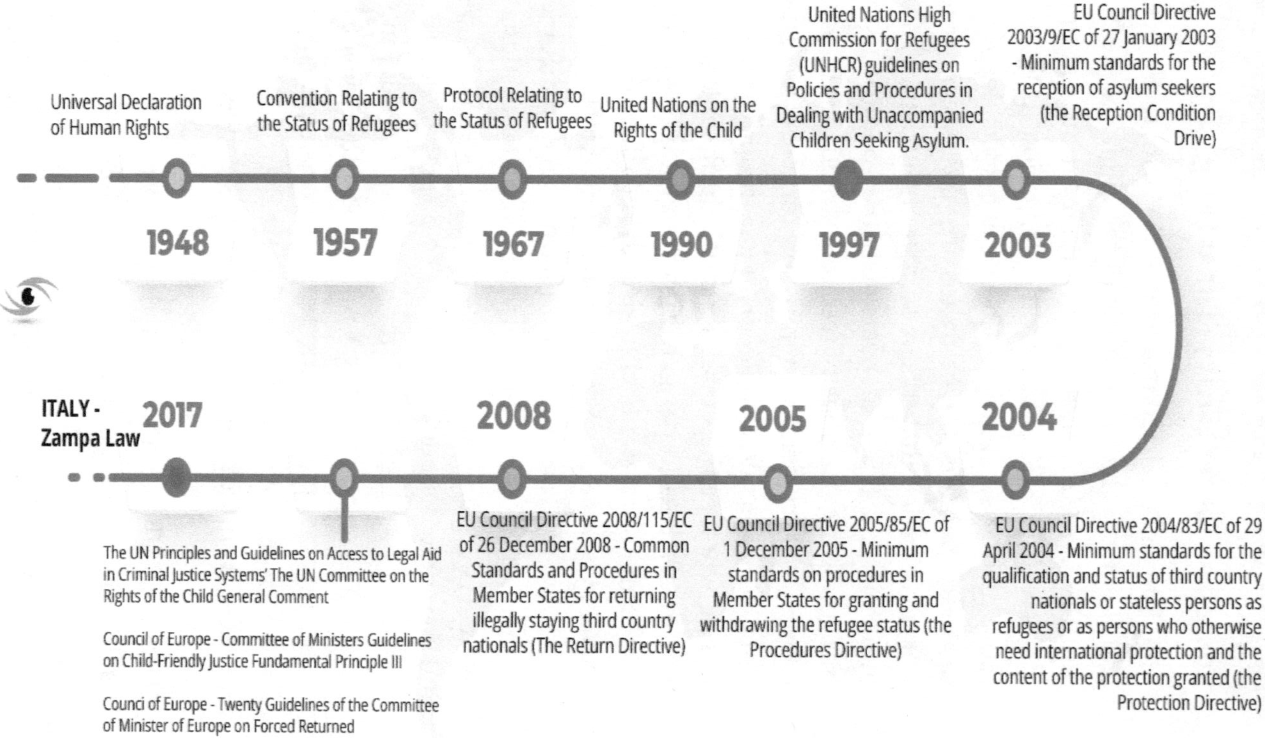

Convention for the Safety of Life at Sea

The International Convention on Maritime Search and Rescue[11], The Convention of the High Seas 1958, and the United Nations Convention on the Law of the Sea (UNCLOS), encode the obligation to rescue those distressed at sea. A sea vessel is considered in distress when it is unworthy to carry passengers or it is so overloaded that it is in danger of capsising. This applies to all types of boats, whether dedicated to mission work, specifically rescuing stranded persons, commercial vessels, warships or cargo ships. The right to be rescued applies to anyone found stranded at sea, whether they intentionally or unintentionally put themselves in danger. This provision has given rise to many migrants choosing to risk their lives to travel by sea, causing an undesired pull effect.

However, according to international maritime law, rescuing stranded persons from international waters is complicated because the law does not stipulate where the persons should be disembarked. The law only provides the seafarers to help the migrants get to safe ground but has no proper guidelines for what this safe place should be. This decision is solely at the discretion of the ship's captain.

This conundrum leaves the vessels between their obligation to basic humane practices and the laws governing the land in which they choose to dock. The ships are sometimes left to wait for long periods in

11 (International Maritime Organization (IMO) 1979)

international waters before they are let into the port to deliver the migrants, especially those who are minors, to get food and medical attention. This causes lengthy delays that disrupt schedules and increase the cost of being at sea. The integrity of the goods aboard the ships, especially the commercial vessels, could also get compromised. According to maritime traditions, when no safe port can be found for the rescuees, the flag states must take responsibility for the rescuees.

United Nations Convention on the Rights of the Child[12]

The 1990 United Nations Convention on the Rights of the child encourages Member States while formulating their policies regarding children to consider the child's best interest. The Convention has forty-one (41) articles, and Article 3 of the Convention guarantees the best interest of the child—The Best Interest of the Child—while Articles 9 and 16 elaborate on family provision for the child and to be represented by a legal representative—Temporary Protection Directive.

Article 11, subsection 4, discourages the trafficking of children and outlines mechanisms that should be put in place to identify, assist and support trafficked minors—Anti-Trafficking Directive. Article 12 discusses the requirements that the child must be given a fair hearing—The Right to be Heard. Article

12 (44/25 n.d.)

20, subsection 1, emphasises the need for separated children to be given special assistance and protection—Special Assistance and Protection for Separated Children.

Furthermore, Article 24 discusses the need for unaccompanied children to be well represented—Recast Reception Conditions Directive—while Article 25 talks about the requirement for children to be represented by legal representatives when attending interviews—Recast Asylum Procedure Directive. Article 37 elaborates on the need for children to be allowed to have legal and other assistance or their liberty is in question—Access to Legal and other Appropriate Assistance in case of the Deprivation of Liberty.

This legal framework, therefore, advocates for the total and unquestioned protection of minors. It also recommends that a guardian is provided to help them access legal assistance.

The Universal Declaration of Human Rights[13]

This is an encompassing human rights document drafted by the United Nations General Assembly, representing members from around the world. The document was adopted on 10 December 1948 in Paris. It has thirty (30) articles that set the universal standard for protecting human rights.[14]

13 (United Nations n.d.)

14 Ibid

The Convention disallows any form of discrimination and supports equality before the law. This means that the rights of unaccompanied minors should be protected without discrimination based on their race, colour, sex, language, religion, political or other opinions, national or social origin, property, birth, or other status.

Under this Convention, all persons, including unaccompanied minors, shall not be subjected to torture or cruel, inhuman or degrading treatment. All human beings, regardless of their age, deserve to be treated in a dignified manner and are recognised as people capable of thoughts and feelings. Unaccompanied migrant minors should be accorded respect and receive the best assistance a situation can provide.

Further, it provides that everyone should be compensated adequately for any acts of violation of human rights guaranteed by the law when appearing before a competent court or tribunals. The unlawful detention or arrest of persons is also highly discouraged.

Most importantly, Article 14 states that everyone has the right to seek and enjoy asylum from persecution in other countries. Further, no one shall be arbitrarily deprived of their nationality nor denied the right to change their nationality. This law, therefore, suggests that migrants are within their rights to seek a change in their nationality and to seek asylum where the need arises.

EU Charter on Fundamental Rights[15]

This legally binding instrument guarantees the fundamental rights of the European Union (EU) Member States. It is an authoritative instrument for policymakers and serves as a human rights litigation source. The instrument has been used to influence the pronouncement of policymakers towards developing human rights laws to meet international standards.[16] The provision of Article 4 prevents unlawful, inhumane torture and undignified treatment of humans, while Article 7 provides for guaranteed access to family.

Article 18 covers the guaranteed rights of asylum seekers under the Geneva Convention of 1951. This is further compounded by the provisions of Article 19 that state that no one shall be expelled to another state where it is believed to be risky or where they can be sentenced to death. This Article guarantees that migrant minors who arrive and are taken into safe countries' borders should not be relocated to a place where their well-being is not guaranteed.

Article 20 guarantees equality of persons before the law, while Article 21 guarantees fair treatment of persons. Moreover, Article 24 guarantees the rights and the best interest of the child. This ensures that children can express themselves freely, and their views are considered depending on their age and maturity. Children have a universal say in how their

15 (European Union 2000)

16 https://www.opensocietyfoundations.org/briefing-papers/eu-charter-fundamental-rights-what-can-it-do

matters are handled, even in a foreign country.

Article 36 provides for a high level of human health protection ensured in the definition and implementation of all Union policies and activities. This also advises on how migrants entering the Union's territory should be treated by medical professionals. Article 41 guarantees the smooth administration of justice in the treatment of children.

European Convention on the exercise of children's rights

The target of this Convention is to support children's rights concerning family actions before the court. The court or the legal representative appointed on behalf of the child may legally represent them before the court and perform all other duties designated to him or her in the child's defence.

This Convention came into force on 1 July 2000, and its main purpose is to serve and guide the child's interests. The Convention consists of certain steps to be taken to enforce and exercise child rights. Furthermore, the Convention has twenty-six (26) articles[17]. Chapter 2 provides the elements that guarantee the steps to be taken to protect children's rights, while Article 15 promotes the reunion between disintegrated families. Similarly, Article 5 covers the guarantees of the rights and best interest of the child, while Article

17 (Council of Europe 1996)

10, Subsection 1, provides for assistance to a child. Going further, Article 13, Subsection 4, provides free legal support for the child and Article 13 provides aid for child victims of trafficking.

Articles 14 and 15, Subsections 3, provides for assistance for children who are trafficked during criminal proceedings. In the same vein, Article 25, Subsection 4, gives unaccompanied minors access to a legal representative and legal information, while Article 21 lists the conditions to be fulfilled in getting legal assistance by the child. Additionally, Article 20 provides for free assistance on legal appeals. Within this framework, the minor is accorded the opportunity for reunification with their family through receiving whatever assistance they may require. The minor should be provided legal representation especially in cases where they are victims of trafficking.

European Union (EU) Dublin III Regulation

This instrument is also known as Regulation EU No 604/2013 of the European Parliament and the Council of 26 June 2013[18]. The regulation provides for the requirements and means for identifying Member States in charge of receiving and investigating requests for international protection in the Member States by Third-Country States. In this case, Member states refer to one of the 'Dublin countries' and include the 28 European Union countries of which

18 (UK Goverment Home Office 2020)

Italy is a member and four countries 'associated' with the Dublin Regulation (Norway, Iceland, Switzerland, and Liechtenstein).

The EU Dublin Regulation (EC 604/2013) replaced the obsolete EU Regulation (343/2003).[19] The regulation has forty-nine (49) Articles.[20] Article 4, subsection 3, provides unaccompanied minors with common information, while Article 6 guarantees the rights and best interests of the child. Moreover, Article 27, subsections 5 and 6, gives unaccompanied minors access to legal representation, legal information, and legal remedies.

Pursuant to the regulation, unaccompanied minors seeking asylum in Dublin countries are eligible for the provision of safety and protection. This regulation provides for the unaccompanied minor to be assigned an adult representative to assist the child in the course of due procedure. In this case, the Dublin procedure requires the authorities to establish whether they are responsible for examining the application or whether another country is responsible. This procedure is made possible by providing accurate information, where possible, by the minor to establish if they have familial or otherwise ties in another country in the Dublin area.

According to the Dublin regulation, the assigned representative ensures that the minor's best interests are a primary consideration, meaning that their needs,

19 (Office of the Refugee Applications Commissioner (ORAC) 2013)

20 Ibid

safety, well-being, social development and views are considered. The representative will also take into account family reunification possibilities. The regulation requires the representative to ensure that the unaccompanied minor is safe and secure, especially from people that may want to treat them badly/ do them harm; they should also make sure that the minor in their care grows up safe and healthy, that they have food and shelter and that their social development needs are met. Lastly, the authorities and the representative must consider the minor's views, for example, whether they would like to stay with a relative or would prefer not to do so.

According to the Dublin procedure, a medical practitioner will assess the unaccompanied minor to ascertain their true age. This is to rule out that they are not older than eighteen since children and adolescents are accorded different treatment. The minor should provide any identification documents, if they have any, to assist in the authentication of their identity. The next step involves the processing of fingerprints. This is a requirement for asylum seekers older than 14 years old. The fingerprints are then entered into a database that will be available for ten years if their application is successful. This step helps the authorities identify if the minor has been fingerprinted at a border. The European Police Office (Europol) may search the fingerprints and request access to the Eurodac database to prevent, detect, and investigate serious crimes and terrorism.

The last step in the procedure is an interview in a language the child understands. The unaccompanied minor is asked to provide information about themselves to establish the next steps regarding their asylum status. The child should not be detained during the period of determination.

The United Nations Sustainable Development Goals (SDGs)

The international legal frameworks are in tandem with the United Nations Sustainable Development Goals (SDGs)[21], which are the world's shared plan to end extreme poverty, protect the planet, and reduce inequality globally by 2030. One hundred and ninety-three countries adopted the fifteen-year plan due to inclusive and comprehensive negotiations that brought together people from across cultures, geographies, and sectors. The stakeholders agreed to put in concerted efforts to achieve the set-out goals to generate the intended impact. The 17 development goals include reduced inequalities, gender equality, zero hunger, and quality education. Resident coordinators, the designated representatives of the Secretary-General for development at the country level, drive the transformation. They coordinate the UN Sustainable Development Group (UN SDG) agencies, funds, and programmes working on development, also known

21 (UN Department of Economic and Social Affairs 2015)

as the UN Country Teams.

The goals are also directly intended to improve the quality of life for children globally. The SDGs are aimed at stemming mortality for children under five, reducing HIV transmission, and ensuring children get proper nutrition. Another key indicator of the development goals for children is improved access to education. This is going to be tracked through the number of students who are enrolled and complete their education from pre-primary through primary and secondary levels. The SDGs are also designed to track gender equality and protection from violence and harmful environments. The plan is geared toward reducing early marriages, violent disciplinary actions, child labour and female genital mutilation.

Another key indicator for the United Nations Sustainable Development Goals is providing children with a safe, clean environment. Children should have access to clean, unpolluted air, safe drinking water, and access to sanitation and hygiene. This also includes using renewable and clean energy sources to promote the protection of the planet for generations to come.

The Sustainable Development Goals, through the drive to leave no one behind, are a crucial opportunity to realise children's rights globally. It will give a fair chance at a better life for children most discriminated against and living in vulnerable situations worldwide. These children include those who are forced by circumstances to live on the streets and in institutions.

The goals also aim to make the lives of children in migration situations easier and free of violence and poverty. Additionally, progress can be accelerated by prioritising children's rights in action plans on the SDGs, as a child rights-based approach multiplies future development gains.

The Sustainable Development Goals call out to all countries, regardless of their stage in development, to promote the prosperity of their citizens while protecting the planet. The goals bring together states to alleviate poverty and promote economic growth. The goals are aimed at addressing a range of social needs, such as social protections and the creation of job opportunities. The SDGs aspire to create a bright future for children. The children themselves are being empowered to be activists for their own needs and to play a role in pushing for the implementation of the SDGs in their countries. This ensures that the children own the process and challenge the adults with new perspectives. The children can be encouraged by allowing them to express their views orally or through art and starting social media campaigns. The children can also be engaged in planting trees to conserve the environment and fight climate change. This ensures that the lessons are passed on and are lived as a reality in the present rather than a goal for the future.

CHAPTER THREE

Italian History and National Laws

ITALY IS A EUROPEAN COUNTRY that boasts rich fertile volcanic soils supporting crops such as grapes and olives. The Italian flag has three colours: vertical strips of red, white, and green. This mountainous country occupies a peninsula that juts into the Mediterranean sea. The unique expanse of wilderness in the lower-lying wilderness hosts a wide range of species rarely seen elsewhere in Western Europe, such as wild boars, wolves, asps, and bears.

Due to the country's rugged terrain, few direct roads exist between its towns and cities. This informs the socio-political geography of the country since the individual regions had to develop a system of independence and self-sufficiency. The political and cultural landscape has been shaped by periods of unification and long separation marked by failed empires and inter-communal strife. The unification occurred in the 19th Century and has since bred a strong, prosperous country known for its rich art and strong economy driven by tourism and trade.

Regionally, the country is part of the European Union and is subject to the statutes that govern the countries therein. The capital city of Italy is Rome. Many tourists visit the city for its famous art. The country is also home to the city of Milan, which is said to be the industrial and fashion centre. Another important part of the country is Vatican City, the independent state that is the seat of the Roman Catholic church and has a predominantly Catholic population.

Italy has a rich history, dating back to the expansive Roman Empire founded in 27 BC. When the empire broke down after the assassination of Julius Caesar, there were many autonomous kingdoms and city-states, and Italy was among them. The Italian Republic was formed in 1946.

Italy joined Austria-Hungary and Germany in the First World War to form the Allies. In 1922, Benito Mussolini overthrew the king and led the country into World War Two. At first, the country was neutral, but Mussolini eventually joined forces with Adolf Hitler of Germany. The lack of resources to launch and sustain the conquering of territories spread Italy's efforts thin, and the nation ended up in chaos. Mussolini was captured and lost the support of Germany. After the war, Italy rebuilt its economy through loans from the Marshall Plan, becoming a strong supporter of the now European Union, and joined the North Atlantic Treaty Organisation (NATO). The Marshall Plan, instituted with the help of the United States, changed the traditional ideas of craftsmanship, frugality, and thrift of the Fascist Era that ushered Italy into the era of modern industrialisation leading to a post-war economic boom. Italy faced several phases of political violence in the late 20th Century leading to the bombing and assassinations of key political figures.

Despite the political upheavals, Italy boasts a rich cultural environment for its people that adopt elements passed down from history with a touch of modernity. The constitution guarantees the freedom of art, science, and teaching. This is evident in its high uptake in education, characterised by enrolment in primary, secondary, and tertiary institutions, especially among the younger generations.[22]

The post-unification era has seen a more cohesive cultural identity due to the uniform education curriculum, mass media, and further integration into the European Union. Italy is famous for its cuisine consisting of the heavy use of grain to make pasta and olive oil.

With an area of 301,340 sq km, Italy is the EU's third most populous member state. The country's immediate neighbours are Austria, France, Slovenia, Switzerland and the independent city-state, the enclaved microstates of Vatican City and San Marino. These countries have shaped the history and foreign policies enshrined in the Italian governing laws. Italy was admitted to the United Nations in 1955. It is a

22 (Pianta 2020)

member and a strong supporter of a wide number of international organisations, such as the Organisation for Economic Co-operation and Development (OECD), the General Agreement on Tariffs and Trade/World Trade Organization (GATT/WTO), the Organization for Security and Co-operation in Europe (OSCE), the Council of Europe, and the Central European Initiative.[23] As a major player in the Mediterranean region, the decisions made in the Italian parliament have far-reaching ripple effects. As such, when Italy makes decisions regarding unaccompanied minors entering its borders, it serves as a gateway towards their passage into the neighbouring states. Should they refrain from taking in migrants rescued at sea, the burden then falls on other coastal states such as France, which often breeds contention.

To stem gross malpractice, especially where international relations are concerned, the Italian Constitution is the supreme binding document ensuring that the government cannot infringe on the inherent rights of persons within its borders. The constitution also determines how laws are made and details the process by which the government rules. The constitution also provides for remedies for unconstitutional acts. Every constitutional framework, whether flexible or rigid, benefits greatly from the addition of by-laws adapted to the changing times to cater for unprecedented situations such as an upsurge of unaccompanied migrants.

23 (French Documentation 2013)

The Italian Constitution provides the legal base for public authorities' administration and is the country's fundamental law of the legal system. Promulgated in 1947, the constitution is written and composed of 139 Articles. The Italian Constitution is rigid, requiring a complex process to amend it. However, the original text has been amended or repealed severally since its promulgation by constitutional laws passed by a special parliamentary procedure. The Italian Zampa law is one such constitutional amendment.

While the Italian Constitution allows for the decentralisation of powers to local authorities, the state reigns supreme. The president, the commander-in-chief of the armed forces, is elected by the parliament. The president has political authority and can authorise the introduction of bills by the government. He also can Promulgate laws, decrees and regulations and ratify international treaties approved in advance by Parliament. It is evident, therefore, that the presidency has a hand in the country's affairs, including the handling of asylum seekers, some of whom are unaccompanied migrant minors.

The constitution of Italy sets out immutable provisions that set out fundamental principles governing the rights of its citizens and their protection. In Article 3, the constitution recognises and grants a person's dignity and the social dignity of all citizens who are considered equal before the law with no distinction. All citizens have a right to work, travel, assemble, profess faith, and express personal thoughts. All persons are at liberty to have a family, acquire education and access to free medical care. The constitution also protects the right of asylum to people who are denied the effective exercise of their democratic freedoms in their own country.

According to Article 117, legislative powers vested in the Italian parliament must comply with the EU legislation and international obligations. Any law that contradicts the rights recognised by an international treaty is considered unconstitutional. Therefore, the Italian Constitution conforms to international standards on asylum seekers. It provides that the state's legislative powers can be exercised for the purpose of immigrant and asylum seekers' legal rights, irrespective of their status.[24]

Due to the rigid nature of the Italian Constitution, the process of amendment or repeal is complicated. The legislative system in Italy is bicameral, meaning that it has two houses of parliament. For a bill to pass, it has to go through both the Chamber of Deputies and the Senate of the Republic. A bill that originates from the House of Deputies must go through the Senate before being passed by the president. In the case of a bill that originates in the Senate, it must be tabled before the House of Deputies and then to the president before it is gazetted as law. A proposed bill will bounce back and forth between the two houses until the document's wording has been agreed upon before

24 (Constitution n.d.) Article 56-58 Constitution of the Republic of Italy

the president can approve it. The process of law formation is established in the Parliamentary Procedure Rules and the Italian Constitution.

The Italian Constitution allows for various methods by which a proposal may reach the parliamentary houses. One way is by a citizen's petition. The petitioner must collect 50,000 signatures to support the proposal. Another way a proposal can be made is through a direct presentation by a member of the Senate of the Republic or the House of Deputies. Also, the five Italian regions may come together to make a joint proposal for a new law. It is the mandate of the Committee of the National Health and Safety Tribunal to make requests for the introduction of a new law. Lastly, the ruling government may propose a new law to create new laws or make amends for existing ones. All these actions point to a democratic system of government and a constitutional process that allows for growth in the judicial process.

The Constitutional Amendment Procedure

The procedure for introducing a bill proposal undergoes several phases in its journey for approval into law. The first phase is the Legislative initiative. When a bill is submitted to the chamber of deputies by the government, it is called a definitive bill, while all others are referred to as proposals of laws. The second phase involves transferring the approved text to the next chamber for approval or amendment. The third step involves sending the amended bill to the other chamber for approval of an identical version. While the proposed bill begins to undergo the flow between the two parliament houses, it is debated by a special parliamentary committee that discusses the proposed bill and prepares a report that is then tabled to the rest of the house members. When the text report has been presented and discussed by the chosen members of parliament, each provision of the bill is examined, and a vote is held on the amendments to the text prepared by the Committee.

The next step is the promulgation by the president if the bill is ready for final approval. However, the president at this stage would be within his/her rights to send the proposal back to the chambers for re-evaluation. The proposed law will therefore have to start the process all over again. This stage is reached when both houses have agreed and approved the proposed bill's contents, suggestions, and wording.

Finally, the law is gazetted. This puts the new law or amendment in the public domain. No referendum is needed when the bill has passed and has been approved by the mandatory number of votes in the parliamentary chambers. At this point, the law is effected and is mandatory for all citizens. The date of the law is that of the decree of promulgation, and its number is that of its insertion into the Official Collection.

Push and Pull Ecosystem in Migration

As of July 2021, the highest number of unaccompanied migrant children in Italy were aged 17 years, tallying at 5,400. In addition, children aged up to six years were 21, representing the smallest group. The migrant situation in Italy has been deteriorating yearly due to external factors such as war and conflict in other countries and continents surrounding Italy.

Minors find their way to Italy, hoping for a better life. However, the situation in most Reception Centres is unsanitary, and the rooms are crowded, barely enough to accommodate the large numbers. Their status also means that they cannot work or study. The process for unification with their families is also long and tedious. For this reason, their stay at the Reception Centres is uncertain, and most end up running away. This is because, according to the law, they cannot be detained.

Those who leave the Reception Centres' sanctuary end up as undocumented minors living in the streets. These minors try to earn money through undeclared work, petty crime, drug trafficking, or prostitution. Living on the streets is difficult because there is no way of getting necessities such as food and sanitation. Minor reprieve is provided by charity organisations and churches that provide warm food and blankets once in a while. However, street children are in danger of drowning, kidnapping or being hit by cars. Those who manage to make it to the Northern parts of Italy apply for asylum in other countries. However, the neighbouring countries are wary of taking them in. Some people take advantage of these migrant minors by beating them up and stealing whatever little money they may have. Others may ask for payment with a promise to smuggle them into other countries only to leave them stranded at the border or in other unknown places. The situation is worsened by policies that seem to encourage the closing of shelters.

The migrant crisis in Italy has been encouraged by certain factors that have determined the increased desire for people to leave their home country or migrate to the country. These are called pull and push factors. The pull factors are those that bring people towards the safe haven that is Italy. One of the pull factors is access to employment, education, and medical care. This is the desired state of well-being for many people in countries where poverty runs high and systems do not work. The migrants are pushed from their own countries by the lack of proper facilities, thus venturing out to seek a better life in Italy.

Migrants are also pulled towards Italy by the desire to gain political freedom. Many countries neighbouring the European country have governments that are not ruled in a democratic manner. Therefore, citizens who hold dissenting opinions often fall prey to mistreatment and even detention. Therefore, they seek asylum in countries like Italy to free themselves from the fear in their home countries and achieve basic freedoms like expression and the right to assembly. Migrants may also move to Italy in search of better environmental conditions as opposed to floods or droughts in their countries of origin.

The push and pull ecosystem in migration is also aided by networks that facilitate the demand and supply of the needs of the migrants. While a migrant may need a better education and lifestyle, they may be unable to get across to another country because they cannot access it, either by sea or by land. Therefore, the ability for migrants to cross the Mediterranean Sea from their countries onto the islands of Italy becomes an enabling factor that facilitates migration. It is also probable that migrants find Italy a safe place to run to because the country has laws that facilitate entry and passage into other European nations. The Italian non-governmental organisations are also known to rescue people from the sea, and those daring enough may risk their lives for a chance to be rescued.

When the migrant crisis began, Italy welcomed asylum seekers with open arms from all countries where people needed help. Italian boats were at the forefront of rescuing drowning persons at sea. However, this hospitality saw the migrants coming in huge numbers. Soon, the Italian people began to feel threatened, and it is rumoured that an element of racism and xenophobia swept across the country. The public then pushed for Italy to stop rescuing people at sea and close its borders. However, the migrants still find their way in, being smuggled into small villages away from the legal border entry points. Most of the work of ensuring that the laws governing migrants entering Italy are followed falls on immigration officers and other law enforcement bodies such as police officers.

Law enforcement officers at the borders are responsible for screening anyone coming in on boats through the seaports. They are also the first line of contact with the ships that contact the maritime officers to seek permission to exit international waters into the Italian territory on the Mediterranean waters. When they are denied permission to dock, they must then decide whether to continue with the journey and take the migrants elsewhere or to wait it out, both situations bearing repercussions on the rescuers.

Law enforcement officers must also deal with the increasing numbers of illegal migrant minors smuggled into the country. They must ensure that the minors are taken to Reception Centres and processed through the immigration process. The officers are also tasked with arresting migrant minors who drug traffickers use to move substances into and around the country. Traffickers use migrant minors and women because the law tends to be more sympathetic to how they are handled.

Immigration officers also work in liaison with other bodies put in place to organise the repatriation and deportation of migrants where need be. They also accompany minors who are set to be reunited with their families in the European Union region.

For many migrant minors, getting to Italy is the end of the journey. For others, it is just the beginning.

For many asylum seekers that arrive on Italy's shores, the legal procedures are too lengthy, and many migrant minors are lost before the end of the process. Getting to the border is half the battle; getting a foothold here is another.

Sometimes the migrant minors often find themselves in the care of non-governmental organisations. These organisations lobby for funding to provide medical care, shelter, food, transportation, and legal services that assist unaccompanied migrant minors through the procedure. The non-governmental organisations run operations in the seas where they charter boats that rescue the migrants at sea and bring them ashore.

However, the place of non-governmental organisations (NGOs) in the migrant crisis, some of which belong to church-based institutions, has been contentious. The organisation lobby for funding to further a humanitarian cause. This move has led to an increase in the uptake of migrants into the country. The NGOs argue that they are stepping in to bridge the gap left by the government institutions when they cannot care for everyone, especially the most vulnerable such as unaccompanied minors. They also help provide a safe place for unaccompanied minors to be kept since the Reception Centres do not have adequate resources. The non-governmental organisations offer a solution for minors who need to be looked after since they cannot be legally detained.

The role of non-governmental and faith-based

organisations in the migrant crisis has also been termed a pull factor for migrants. When migrants believe they can take to the sea, be rescued by the boats, and be ferried into Italy, many are encouraged to take the dangerous journey.

The question of civil society's involvement in the migrant crisis brings up underlying migratory policy issues. There has been no legislation in the European Union that stipulates who is legitimately concerned with the issue of migrants who take to the sea to seek asylum in the Dublin area. Further, civil society is mandated to advocate for the rights of minorities and the vulnerable. Therefore, there is a push and pull between the sanctity of preserving the lives of those who would be lost to unsafe sea travel and government directives aimed at curbing a migrant problem.

Even more problematic is the role of the media in highlighting the migrant crisis. What people read in the news or watch on television has been found to influence their opinions and beliefs heavily. The media has been used repeatedly to shift political opinion in favour of one party. Therefore, the media bears great responsibility in how they choose to address the migrant crisis. When the media terms the migrants as pollutants, the societal treatment of the newcomers shifts to view them as problems or irritants that should not be treated humanely but instead gotten rid of. Using terms that alienate the migrant separates the masses from the migrants. This makes the situation appear to be a security issue rather than a humanitarian one. The citizens then are less likely to want to help the migrants, whether children or adults. Addressing the matter in the news as being a burdensome, costly affair to taxpayers reduces the human cost suffered by asylum seekers in Italy.

To even out the ground for migrant minors, it was necessary to create a uniform procedure at the national level for age verification and identification of minors. This kind of law would provide a structured system of reception of unaccompanied minors into the country. The law would ensure that the best interest of the minor and inherent rights such as access to education and health are protected. It was important to create an Italian Law that would grant minors access to legal aid and to be heard in any judicial and administrative procedures that they are involved in. This situation necessitated the inception of the Zampa Law to protect the unaccompanied child.

An unaccompanied child, according to Italian law, is *'a minor who is not a national of Italy or any other EU Member State and who has not presented an application for political asylum and for any reason is in the territory of the State without assistance and representation from parents or other adults legally responsible'.*

Laws made in any country are reflections of the moral beliefs that people live up to. Globally, existing laws regulate the action and general welfare of its people and the country itself. These laws are meant to protect all persons fairly and equitably. The inception of this law speaks to a government's dedication to protecting the rights of unaccompanied minors in its borders and is fair to the taxpayers as it stipulates that no extra expenditure would go into its implementation.

Italy has several laws that apply to unaccompanied migrant minors, particularly regarding guardianship, as elaborated below. These include:

- Law 142/2015 as amended by DL 220/2017, which came into force in January 2018, L.4/05/1983 no. 184, Dlgs; and
- 25/08, T.U. immigrazione Dlgs 286/98 and Law 47/2017 also known as the Zampa Law.

Italian Zampa Law

The Zampa Law is a new legislation that guarantees and protects the rights of unaccompanied minors in Italy. The Italian Parliament debated the bill for four years, after which it was passed into law on 28 March 2017 and came into force in 2018. The principal purpose of the new law is to protect the rights and prescribe standards on how unaccompanied minors are treated in Italy.[25]

The content of the law includes: '*Age assessment and identification of Unaccompanied Minors; establish a structured national reception system, with minimum standards in all reception facilities; attention to the best*

25 (Zandonini 2017)

interests of the child; education and health rights; the right to be heard in administrative and judicial proceedings about unaccompanied minors, even in absence of a guardian, and legal assistance.'[26]

Articles 1 and 2 of Zampa Law 47/2017 state as follows: *"The President of the Republic promulgates the following law: Art. 1 Unaccompanied foreign minors are holders of rights in Protection of minors at equal treatment with the Minors of Italian citizenship or of the European Union. 2. The provisions of this Act shall apply to unaccompanied foreign minors because of their condition of greater vulnerability."*

Article 2 defines unaccompanied minors by giving recognition to children and teenagers. Article 3 disallows refoulement, while Article 5 lays down the steps for regulating the identification process for unaccompanied children. Furthermore, Articles 6 and 8 discuss how family investigations and repatriation should be handled, whereas Article 7 mandates local authorities to encourage foster care instead of false imprisonment. Articles 14 and 17 give an unaccompanied child the right to access health services and schooling.

The Zampa Law has been effective in some ways by filling in the gaps in the Italian immigration service system. The law advocates for group efforts instead of the enforcement of minors. This law was highly praised by UNICEF and the European Council Refugees and Exiles for the revision and as a model

26 (Minorisna 2017)

for other European countries. Among the changes made as provided under Zampa Law is that children cannot be held for more than thirty (30) days at the Reception Centers, unlike the former sixty (60) days plus additional ten (10) days meant for identification and age verification.

Furthermore, The Zampa Law also made provision for professionals to help the unaccompanied migrant minors, as well as psychologists, cultural mediators, legal advisors, and short-term volunteer guardians. Regional officials are in charge of training the volunteer guardians on how to interact with minors and teenagers. Each minor is entitled to an adult representative within three months of arrival. Similarly, the minors will also be guided and informed of all the necessary procedures to take the asylum process by the cultural mediator, including appeals.

After that, the children are taken to the Protection System for Refugees and Asylum Seekers (SPRAR) in Italy. According to Zampa Law, these structures mentioned in the new law are meant solely for unaccompanied migrant minors.

In addition, a database has also been created by a Social Folder called Cartella Sociale, which will be used to monitor the whereabouts of the unaccompanied minors and assist the volunteer guardians in determining the exact needs of the minors to satisfy their future plans. The Zampa Law also gave unaccompanied migrant minors access to the National Healthcare Service (SSN) before the assignment of guardianship and special agreements for apprenticeships. It subsidised mandatory school for unaccompanied migrant minors.

Moreover, amendments were made to the family investigations and support provisions for assisted repatriations under the new law. Currently, International Organization for Migration (IOM) foresees affairs of family investigations whilst the General Department for Immigration at the Juvenile Court, an expert that looks at the child's best interest, manages the assisted repatriations. Another feature of the new law is the creation of a list of volunteer guardians within three months for unaccompanied migrant minors to be represented by an adult. Although, in the previous immigration procedure for the appointment of guardians, the process for selection in all Reception Centers, especially in the first reception stage, is not the same.[27] The volunteer guardians are selected and undergo training by regional ombudspersons for teenagers and children.

The new law mandated the local authorities to support foster care instead of only accommodation in the Reception Centres. It also encourages the implementation of two types of residence permits—for unaccompanied migrant minors and family—substituted for integration, permits for fostering, and pending fostering requests which are normally used by common practices or never used at all.

The new legislation also introduces safeguards

27 (Defense for Children International Italia OdV n.d.)

such as the rights to participate and the appointment of a representative through administrative or judicial proceedings in line with recent law while helping the minor along the stages. In addition, under Article 17, the new law provides for a special assistance program for unaccompanied migrant minors who are victims of trafficking through protection and guidance.

Once a law is gazetted, it remains to be enacted and applied to common practice. The Zampa Law particularly is meant to cater to the rights of unaccompanied minors. The minor will come into contact with the judicial process through the help of their chosen guardian, who will serve as both a representative and an interpreter of how the system works. With its language and logic, the judicial world is very intimidating to a child. And depending on the child's age, they may be in no position to understand it at all. This may leave the child feeling alienated and lost. However, having a guardian allows the child to comprehend how the system is tailored to their needs and rights. This has a better and more positive outcome overall to the assimilation and perception of the procedures involved in their transition to life in the country.

The new law ensures that migrant minors can participate in, accept, and understand the results of judicial proceedings. The Zampa Law provides for legislation that is compliant with European and National legislation but is adapted to the minors' specific needs for their well-being. When minors feel that they can communicate and express their opinions, they are more likely to feel less anxious about the sudden changes in their circumstances.

In order to assimilate the child in their judicial process, it is necessary for all persons involved in the legal aid of the child to adopt the use of child-friendly language. This kind of age-appropriate communication promotes the rights of migrant minors to participate in the proceedings. This, therefore, upholds the values enshrined in the Zampa Law and the Italian Constitution.

The unified judicial system of Italy should ensure that no child slips through the cracks. The system should ensure that each case is handled fairly and that the Zampa Law benefits the unaccompanied minors for whom it is meant.

The implementation of every law presents its own special set of challenges that hinder the process of execution. Some common challenges that may hinder the rollout of the policies enshrined in the new law include the lack of political goodwill in subsequent governments and economic crises. Political goodwill can affect the application of a law where the agendas of the ruling party do not highlight the plight of unaccompanied minors. Economic recessions and upheavals may leave the government in a situation where they cannot maintain the systems required to process and protect unaccompanied minors.

The process may also be hindered by the lack of goodwill on the part of the masses. This would affect the volunteering process through which the guardians are made available for the minors. The volunteer guardians may feel too intimidated to engage with the systems that seek to ensure that the unaccompanied minor is protected.

The lack of accountability may also hinder policies and stipulations enshrined in the Zampa Law. In the case where no one is in charge of making sure that the processes for identification and psychological assessment are done in a timely and professional manner, many children will continue to get lost in the cracks. This will result in the same state of lawlessness that existed before the law came into being. A lack of accountability may also see funds meant to support the machinery involved in the child's welfare diverted to other things. Therefore, the quality of care that the unaccompanied minor receives would be subpar and take much longer than necessary.

The execution of the law may also encounter challenges when trying to authenticate the child's information. The process of reaching out to their guardians may be hindered, and they will not get the chance to appeal.

CHAPTER FOUR

THE GUARDIAN

VIOLA AND HER SISTER VIOLET are both signed up as volunteer guardians. Viola first got into guardianship when she met Yusuf, a young man, in the hospital. Yusuf was only thirteen and in hospital after a grisly road accident. Yusuf was living on the streets at the time. He had been taken in by other undocumented migrants who lived that way. Yusuf had ended up on the streets after running away from a reception centre. The process for processing and paperwork was long and tedious. Additionally, Yusuf did not know a single word in Italian.

Viola was moved to helping Yusuf at first glance. She, a mother, imagined what it would be like for one of her children to end up in a foreign country alone. She approached the young man and began to interpret the world to him; she found that she was naturally adapted to the role as she explained things to her children every day. She helped Yusuf get through the asylum-seeking process and attempted to reunite the minor with his family.

Violet got into guardianship much later after seeing how her sister had impacted the life of the teenage unaccompanied minor she assisted. They are now part of Italy's volunteer guardianship program, established in 2017 after the adoption of the Zampa Law. The sisters, alongside other volunteers, protect vulnerable migrant children from abuse and trafficking. Besides being involved in their asylum process, the guardians can serve as long-life mentors and dream shapers. The guardian must facilitate the entry and attendance of schools and medical consults.

The institution of legal guardians was instituted in Italy alongside the promulgation of the Zampa Law. The institution was created because the government felt that the guardians formally appointed and hired by the government were not as effective. Therefore, the need for voluntary guardians to take responsibility for unaccompanied foreign minors became necessary. The voluntary guardians receive special training before interacting with unaccompanied minors. This improves their capacity to protect the child and guide them through the required processes.

Definition and Role of a Guardian

A guardian is an independent individual who protects a child, looks out for their best interests and welfare and assists them in enhancing their capabilities and working on their weaknesses. The guardian may also perform roles similar to the parents as a legal representative in all courts and administrative proceedings.[28] The concept of an effective guardianship system cannot be overstressed to prevent abuse, exploitation and neglect. Therefore, having a guardian representing unaccompanied children would better protect and secure the child's future. However, it is to be noted that each guardianship capability, experience, and educational background differs among Member states.

According to the Asylum Information Database (AIDA), a guardian is a person engaged by the government to provide legal capacity to minors who have no relatives abroad. They are also responsible for providing them with protection and shelter and assisting them in processing their documents. To be qualified as a legal guardian, they must be free from criminal records, professional in the job, and comply with the terms and conditions specified for the job as a guardian. In addition, the guardian must also be capable of taking adequate care of the child in their custody. Furthermore, it is also imperative to recognise the child's culture regarding religion, language, and colour to allow for free communication between them.

The guardian must be able to guide the minor in their care through the various processes required of

28 (COMMITTEE ON THE RIGHTS OF THE CHILD 2005)

asylum seekers. The process may take long as Italian law doesn't allow unaccompanied minors access to the accelerated procedure that takes nine days. This is because the cases of unaccompanied minors need to be handled delicately alongside those of people with special needs, which should coincide with vulnerable people as identified by Article 17 of the Reception Decree.[29]

The guardian must be able to explain to the minor what it means when their application for asylum or reunification with their families has been accepted or rejected. They also need to help the child transition through the procedures required when they need to be transferred to another country in the Dublin area where their application will be processed.

According to Italian law, the guardian must work alongside other officers involved in the procedure. The guardian will be able to create a buffer between the child and the authorities to protect their rights. The guardian will likely encounter the child after the border police have already processed them at the point of entry when they are rescued from the boat. The immigration police will then transfer the minor to the reception centre. They are also involved in the interviews needed to get information on the child's origin and interests. In the case of any appeals in the procedure, the guardian may accompany the minor to court hearings.

---

29 (AIDA Database 2022)

An effective guardian can assist the child in obtaining the documents they are entitled to. These documents include a passport, identification cards, residency, health cards, tax codes, and a permit of stay. The acquisition of these documents may involve lengthy processes through which the guardian assists the child. The guardian should also visit the child to evaluate the child's living conditions. As such, the guardian should be able to recommend changes to the living conditions where needed so that the child is safe and adequately taken care of. Additionally, the guardian should listen to the child's views and opinions regarding what interests them. This is not only a constitutional right but also assists the child to follow their passions in the new country, for example, if they would like to join a football club or get training in speciality technical careers.

Guardians must build relationships with the unaccompanied migrant minor in their care in an environment that respects the child's religion, customs, and culture. This ensures that the child feels safe in their own choices and individuality. The guardian should also advise on the decisions that the minor wishes to make. Such choices include matters regarding their schooling. As the child reaches the age of 18 and is no longer a minor, the guardian should be there to ensure that their passage is uneventful and that they establish themselves as productive young adults. This ensures that they do not end up on the streets or in the hands of traffickers.

One of the main objectives of the Zampa Law is to promote foster care and enhance the guardianship system by involving and training locals as volunteer guardians. In Italy, guardianship is voluntary and not remunerated. This allows for a relationship based on affection, trust and mutual enrichment. Relationships between guardians and unaccompanied minors inevitably become long-lasting, far beyond laws and regulations.

The voluntary guardianship model aims to demonstrate that a more humane reception and creating a warm, 'familiar' environment will not only enhance protection but, by engaging locals actively, foster integration in the host community. The model also encourages minors to stay within their foster families or centres versus running away when the process takes too long or becomes tedious. This approach is the basis for a more welcoming, multicultural society that sees the child before the migrant.

The minor-volunteer relationship is, however, riddled with challenges. Most minors come from low-income families and lack access to learning any international languages. Therefore, upon entry to Italy, they cannot understand the language. Therefore, there is a communication barrier between the guardian and the migrant minor. This barrier is crossed eventually as the child is integrated into learning institutions. However, initially, the relationship may rely on the presence of a translator. However, technological tools such as phone applications that can translate what is said back and forth greatly improve the situation without the need for a third party.

The guardian also faces challenges as they attempt to advocate for the rights of the minor. This can include the refusal of the centre to adjust their diet to the special requirement of the migrant minor. This stems from the bureaucracy and red tape surrounding their attempts to gather legal information and progress reports on acquiring the necessary documents.

The Zampa Law in Pioneering Volunteerism

Even before the Zampa Law and its provisions for volunteer guardians, the concept of volunteerism had been recognised for its benefit to society and the individual. Volunteerism is at the heart of human relationships and expressions of solidarity and genuine care. Volunteerism is built on mutual trust, reciprocity, belonging, and empowerment. These values have been found to improve the quality of life significantly. This is the case with volunteer guardians who aim to contribute positively to the lives of unaccompanied migrant minors.

The Zampa Law is pioneering the recognition of the informal role of volunteering towards achieving socioeconomic goals. People worldwide have volunteered to support causes that matter to them, such as improving basic health and tackling environmental issues. One of the most common activities is tree planting, which contributes to combating climate change. Other volunteer opportunities exist in government and non-governmental efforts to provide safe water supplies and sanitation and tackle social exclusion and poverty. This is the cornerstone on which the provision of the Zampa Law is built to engage the help of volunteer guardians to assist the migrant minors in their communities.

Volunteerism has formed the backbone of civil society organisations mainly run on non-profit models and thus cannot afford to pay for the required labour necessary to make an impact. It is also a concept that is increasingly growing in popularity in the private sector. However, in this setup, volunteering is a way to acquire skills that contribute to career growth. Volunteerism is a sustainable service provision because it fosters an environment where individuals dictate their engagement. In this environment, there is less focus on self-interest and competition that would otherwise breed negativity in the workplace. Volunteering provides the opportunity to contribute to the community and improve well-being.

Volunteering benefits not only the community but also the individual. The volunteers are more likely to develop vocal skills and become politically active. Zampa Law intends to create this kind of environment in Italy. Through training the guardians on their role in the lives of the migrant minors, the volunteers can attach more personal importance to serving the public interest. The guardians are empowered to cultivate an outlook that contributes to a social environment that nurtures the well-being of all individuals.

Volunteer work involves being responsive to the needs of other people. This kind of work helps individuals to appreciate humanity and spiritual well-being. Additionally, the volunteer feels good for changing the course of another's life. This is great for self-esteem. In the long run, volunteers appreciate their place in society and contribute to better mental health. Volunteering can be considered a form of social capital in communities. When everyone is concerned for the well-being of others, cohesion is fostered, thus promoting development. In such an environment, fewer discrimination cases are likely because people work together and respect the other's contribution.

Volunteering helps the individual to interact with others and to make new friends. This is because Volunteerism brings together like-minded people who enjoy sharing and selflessly using their skills for the common good. One's social skills are improved with every interaction. This helps especially the younger people in developing future personal and business relationships. Meeting mentors and making career networks that may inform job prospects is possible during the volunteering activities. The volunteer faces various challenges that require the individual to devise solutions. By exercising critical thinking, the individual assists others and contributes to personal development.

Given the important role that the guardian plays

in the life of the unaccompanied migrant minor, the individual must be vetted appropriately. This is important, alongside the training, to ensure they are up to the task. While anyone can volunteer to be a guardian, it is important that the individual can guide the minor appropriately.

The guardian should also be psychologically prepared to deal with the delicate state of the vulnerable minors. Oftentimes, the migrant minors may lash out or be incredibly withdrawn. This may require extra help from a psychologist. However, the guardian should be equipped to handle the situation independently to care for the child adequately. The volunteers should be able to know and understand the specific rights and needs of child victims of trafficking. Guardians should be capable of assessing their needs and dealing with them respectfully, sensitively, professionally, and in a non-discriminatory manner.

The volunteer must also be morally upright. Volunteerism is based on the institution of mutual trust. Therefore, the volunteer must be someone who can be trusted not to abuse the child in any way. The government should conduct a background check on all volunteers before allowing them to interact with the children. The volunteer needs to be virtuous because the minor will learn how to behave from them. When the child is taught the best way to be a good citizen in the country that they live in, they are more likely to have a productive outlook in the short term and when they become adults.

In terms of suitability, gender plays a huge role. This is especially so for young girls who have been victims of abuse. This particular set of children may require to be matched with a sympathetic female guardian who can help them to feel safe. Guardians are therefore invited to develop an awareness of one's cultural attributes and stereotypes and their impact on one's behaviour and beliefs.

A guardian should be assigned immediately if the child is found to be unaccompanied or separated from their parents or caregivers. The guardian can also be appointed when there is a conflict between the parents and the law and it is deemed unsafe for the child to continue being in the care of their parents. A temporary guardian is appointed in such a situation until the situation is resolved. This is done because the law upholds the well-being and interests of the child as supreme. The child may also be released into the custody of a guardian when it is found that the parents are in some way involved in the trafficking of the child. In such a case, it is unsafe for the child to remain in the care of their parents.

A temporary guardian may be appointed in cases where the child's age is in dispute. However, a person who claims to be a minor will be treated as such until proven otherwise. Therefore, they are assigned a guardian to help them through age verification. Authorities should allow guardians sufficient time to meet and prepare the child before procedures are initiated and decisions are taken. No decisions should be made on behalf of the child before a guardian has been assigned.

The guardianship arrangement naturally ends should the minor be reunified with their parents. A guardian is also not required after the age of 18. However, the relationship may continue informally where the guardian and the assigned migrant minor have bonded and the young adult feels the need to be guided by the guardian. The role of a guardian also ends when the child crosses over to another country. The guardianship may also end when a child runs away from the Reception Centres or foster care and cannot be found. Lastly, the guardian should be stopped from accessing the child should they be under investigation for any form of abuse or for committing a crime.

CHAPTER FIVE

The Present and the Future of the Zampa Law

Under the old Italian Immigration Law in relation to the services provided for unaccompanied minors arriving in Italy, the procedure for identifying minors is not the same due to many different landing points. A report by the European Parliament and the Council of the European Union emphasised some of the challenges encountered by unaccompanied minors and the lack of consistency in how immigration officers interpret registration procedures for unaccompanied migrants entering Italy[30]. The situation encountered by unaccompanied minors arriving in Italy calls for urgent attention. The number of unaccompanied minors doubled in 2016 compared to previous years. In 2015, they were estimated to be 12,360 children and the report for 2016 shows about 25,800. Going by the report by UNHCR in 2017[31], 11,406 unaccompanied

30 (REGULATION (EU) No 516/2014 OF THE EUROPEAN PARLIAMENT AND OF THE COUNCIL 2014)

31 (United Nations High Commissioner for Refugees 2017)

minors have landed on Italian shores. The data was analyzed and interpreted as 92 per cent of these children arrived on the shores of Italy without being accompanied by adults.

Meanwhile, UNICEF had foreseen an increase in the number of accompanied minors moving into Italy. Most of them fall victim to sexual exploitation, rape, and human trafficking. The report indicated that the majority of these minors come from Nigeria.

Furthermore, when these unaccompanied minors arrive on the shores of Italy, either from Libya or Nigeria, they stay unattended at the immigration and Reception Centres. Most of the time, the local police are not organised to carry out the identification processes. Many of the migrants are wrongly identified by the guards at the border because of the high inflow of migrants and the low number of police officers on duty. Some ports are fast to identify these minors, while others are not. For the ports to be able to carry out the recognition mechanism quickly, their fingerprints are immediately taken. Equally, at ports like Pozzallo, photographs of the minors are taken, and the children are immediately transferred to the Reception Centers located in the northern part of Italy, where they will be identified.

The unaccompanied minors encounter other challenges at various ports, including the lack of interpreters and immigration lawyers to assist them in the identification procedures. On several occasions, international organisations like IOM, UNHCR and other

NGOs like Save the Children, Terre des Hommes, and the Italian Red Cross, have tried to intervene and fill the vacuum created by the Italian immigration system. They have assisted the unaccompanied minors by giving guidance and medical treatment.

Additionally, immigration services of the Prefecture believed that migrants are misusing the opportunity of the asylum system. Most of the time, during the registration of the date of birth for unaccompanied minors, some are usually given the wrong birth date, and their names are misspelt on the documents. This is caused by improper translation at interviews in various ports during their arrival. It has been difficult for police officials to determine their real age at that particular moment. This state of affairs has resulted in most unaccompanied minors being registered as adults in ports like Pozzallo, Augusta, and Catania.

Another major challenge encountered in the immigration service is the inability to authenticate any information provided by unaccompanied minors regarding nationality, age, and identity. The minors also use this challenge to manipulate their identity and registration altogether. The European Commission, in December 2015, advised Italy and Greece to consider measures in terms of fingerprints of migrants related to the rule in the Dublin Regulations. Similarly, the European Commission also advised Italy to take records of all fingerprints of migrants in hotspot centres to hasten migrants' movement to other EU countries. The Italian immigration system, however, found it difficult and was reluctant to take a record of disembarking migrant fingerprints. Reports from Borderline Sicily and the Association for Juridical Studies on Immigration (ASGI) showed that migrant minors' fingerprints are obtained against their will at the disembarkation port. There were also reports of human rights violations by the Italian police and the European agency Frontex in charge of hotspot centres. This includes intentionally depriving them of access to Italian cities. As a result of the challenges mentioned above encountered by unaccompanied minors with the Italian immigration service system, there were comments and complaints from the international community and NGOs about the need for Italy to revise its immigration law to consider the best interest of unaccompanied minors arriving in Italy.

The Guardianship Systems and Requirements

The procedure under Italian law for the appointment of a guardian is that they must be nominated within 48 hours. These minors often find it challenging to appeal without a guardian. It is important to emphasise the numerous roles of a legal guardian in assisting unaccompanied minors moving into Italy, which include, but are not limited to, escorting them for an appointment at the immigration office, appearing with the minors at the interview centres as well as helping them to process their asylum claims.[32] When a minor is unable to get a legal guardian, they may be prone to abuse, neglect, exploitation and delayed procedures in the process of their asylum claims. Between 2008 and 2012, there was an increase in the appointment of guardians to unaccompanied migrant minors in Italy[33].

The Current Procedure for the Appointment Of A Guardian

The judicial authorities are charged with the responsibility of appointing a guardian in many cases. However, there are specified rules for the appointment of guardians except the general provisions given by the Civil Code. Judges' decisions can only determine the appointment, which may not be based on the child's best interest.

Furthermore, in the procedure for the appointment of guardians, there are two suggested ways:

- Private volunteers: a person who shows interest and is ready and available to be a guardian.

- Institutional volunteers comprise both natural and legal persons recognised under the law. However, this method

32 (Defense for Children International Italia OdV n.d.)

33 Ibid.

> may only be used as a fallback where it is impossible to use the first method (private volunteer).[34]

The methods mentioned above go together in countries with similar jurisdictions. This method also suggested uniformity in the procedures for the appointment of guardians to remove gaps created within and outside the country. In addition, voluntary guardianship can be used as a tool to generate fairness in appointing guardians and prevent selection biases. The following are the appointment procedures in Milan and Genoa, Italy.

Guardianship Appointment Procedure in Milan

The Tutelary Judge appoints guardians in Milan based on the report and recommendations of the Municipality of Milan's social service department. The department of social service in charge of unaccompanied migrant minors will first determine the condition of the child and make a report to the judicial authority within thirty days of the assessment. During the evaluation, the child is placed in a residential place after a request has been made for guardianship. The usual practice is for the Tutelary Judge to appoint someone to spearhead the guardianship board after taking an oath. Where there are no emergencies, the

34 Ibid

appointment of a guardian may vary. Sometimes, it takes several months.[35]

Additionally, among the categories of people that can act as guardians in Milan are the public officers who perform the duties that have to do with the child's property and administrative matters. The social assistant is responsible for the practical tasks concerning unaccompanied migrant minors. Practically, the terms social assistant and guardian are used interchangeably. Between 50 and 60 unaccompanied migrant minors are usually assigned to social assistance annually. Finally, the Director of Service is in charge of the general supervision of the reception centres in Milan.[36]

The guardians in Milan are responsible for working with organisations or agencies that deal with issues related to unaccompanied migrant minors. They are also responsible for compliance with the international standard—the European standard. The guardian in Milan is responsible for regularly meeting the children's needs. This includes providing the child with their contact number in case of emergency and making themselves accessible to the child to meet their urgent needs. The guardians are regarded as competent professionals. However, they must undergo different training from other professionals in the field of child protection.

35 (Defense for Children International Italia OdV n.d.)

36 Ibid

Guardianship Appointment Procedure in Genoa

Tutelary Judge appointed guardianship in Genoa based on a request from the police headquarters (Questura) for unaccompanied migrant minors. As the guardian would have to process the minor residence permit, their appointment tends to be faster. Guardian appointment is crucial for processing the unaccompanied minor legal status and protective services. The guardianship system started in 2008, and since 2010, the Municipality has handled all requests. Initially, lawyers voluntarily expressed interest in the Tutelary Judge being appointed as a guardian. However, the availability of lawyers became low due to the increase in unaccompanied migrant minors, thus putting unsustainable pressure on the implementation modality. Based on the above, the appointment of a guardian was extended to institutional actors like Heads of Department of the Municipality, who in turn delegate their functions to other subjects like the Public Officers.

The guardians, who are voluntary lawyers, work with other organisations or agencies on matters involving children through informal collaboration. However, the level of coordination becomes weak, and the guardians are not always present during crucial decision-making processes. As a result, other actors assumed some of their responsibilities. The relationship between the guardian and the minor is blurred. The project shows a lack of mutual trust, confidentiality and openness between the minor and the guardian. However, the children tend to develop these relationships with other actors like social workers, social assistants, and, sometimes, cultural mediators. The training of guardians in Genoa was recent, and measures had been taken and put in place by the Municipality to train voluntary guardians for unaccompanied migrant minors. It focused on five topics under the Convention on the Rights of the Child's principles and provisions: European and National legal and normative framework; Mapping of the child protection system and actors; Child development; Psychological listening technique for the minor, and knowledge of migration issues and intercontinental connection.

CONCLUSION

BASED ON THE ABOVE ANALYSIS, it has been noted that there are existing gaps in the Italian immigration law for unaccompanied migrant minors arriving in Italy which is supported by the 2014 report of the European Migration Network, which explained some challenges encountered by unaccompanied migrant minors especially the lack of consistency in the way immigration officers interpret registration procedures for unaccompanied migrant migrants in Italy. In addition, the international community and NGOs also had been complaining about the problems encountered by unaccompanied migrant minors with the immigration service system in Italy. They suggested that Italy should revise its immigration law and consider the best interest of unaccompanied migrant minors arriving on its shores.

In introducing the new Zampa Law, Italy has made incredible changes to help the situation of unaccompanied migrant minors arriving on its shores. The new Zampa Law has introduced new initiatives and innovations to alleviate the challenges encountered in the immigration system. This new law was highly praised by UNICEF and the European Council for Refugees and Exiles, which could serve as a model for other European countries facing the same challenges. The law also fixed many gaps left by the old immigration law for unaccompanied migrant minors by providing them with professional expert support like a psychologist, cultural mediator, legal advisor, and short-term volunteer guardians upon their arrival in Italy.

However, a critical comparison between international law regarding legal guardians and Italy's immigration and reception system for unaccompanied migrant minors shows that the Italian reception system for unaccompanied minors and the guardianship system suffers a lot of setbacks. The Italian immigration and reception system shows that unaccompanied migrant minors are not strongly given adequate protection as they are restricted from being integrated and regularised into the Italian system and territory. Most of the time, they were detained at the border or returned to their countries of origin. Furthermore, the Convention on the Rights of the Child remains a principal international instrument when issues related to a child are involved. As discussed above, the Convention places major responsibilities on State parties to take all necessary steps not to treat a child based on their nationality or legal status but to promote and safeguard the well-being and interest of the child. The Convention has a legal force on all

Member States, including all the European Countries, including Italy, that have ratified it. The Convention ensures that unaccompanied migrant minors are accorded fundamental human rights as provided for. The convention, however, has four general principles that can serve as a guide to Member States. These are reflected under Articles 2, 3, 6 and 12 of the Convention on the Rights of a Child. Article 2 emphasises the principle of non-discrimination; Article 3 elaborates on the elements of the child's best interest; Article 6 highlights the right of the child, survival and development; and Article 12 expresses the component that a child has the right to express their views freely.

Additionally, as provided by the international principles in the appointment and roles of a guardian, the principle is to act in the best interest of unaccompanied migrant minors. All the instruments require that unaccompanied children be accorded a guardian or a representative. Furthermore, each instrument requires that there should be a well-established framework that will consider and act in the best interest of a child. One of the qualities of a guardian, as provided by these international instruments, is that they must have the required expertise and be in charge of the wellness, safety and vulnerability and the development of the child's capability. Moving forward, the guardians are required to deal with the child per their age and maturity, taking into consideration and helping in family tracing and unification. The guardians are also advised to inform the child of the asylum procedures and must ensure that they attend the interviews with the child and provide any relevant assistance and support to the processing of the asylum request. In exercising their duties and responsibilities, the directives encourage the guardians to always work towards the child's best interest.

Furthermore, the Dublin III Regulations also give some important provisions mandating the guardians to act in the best interest of the unaccompanied migrant minors. Moreover, it further states that EU transfer may only be considered where family unity is involved. On the other hand, the Regulations did not mention who is responsible for transferring a child from one EU state to another. To clarify the above issues, there is an urgent need to make clear terms in the regulations and directives which will give a comprehensive and centralized definition of guardianship for unaccompanied children.

The analysis above has shown the various challenges encountered by unaccompanied migrant minors at various ports in Italy due to the lack of a good guardianship system. The unaccompanied migrant minors also experience other challenges, like a lack of interpreters and immigration lawyers to assist them in the identification procedures. This has been traced to the old immigration laws, which failed to provide for a good guardianship system for unaccompanied migrant minors and as well as not meet the international standard.

As mentioned above, a good and effective

guardianship system is highly recognised under the international legal frameworks as provided for under Article 20 of the Convention on the Rights of a Child. It is to be noted that the new Zampa Law has corrected the majority of the issues mentioned above raised for unaccompanied migrant minors in Italy. Although the new Zampa Law has started to become more popular with high recognition in Italy and a benchmark for other European countries, its implementation is being carefully followed by the Italian Government. The provisions under the Zampa Law have provided many options to fix the gaps created by the old immigration service system, thus bringing it up to meet the international standard.[37]

37 (Defense for Children International Italia OdV n.d.)

RECOMMENDATIONS

THE FINDINGS HAVE shown discrepancies in European guardianship practice, characterised by a lack of an effective guardianship system for unaccompanied migrant minors. Italy is our case study, and a few EU Member States are experiencing the same challenges, viz Belgium and the Netherlands. Belgium has a specific law on the guardianship system for unaccompanied, while the Netherlands has a commission set up to precisely and adequately provide guardianship services for unaccompanied minors. However, Italy has no well-structured guardianship system for unaccompanied minors arriving at its borders. However, based on the findings and because the new Italian Zampa Law on unaccompanied migrant minors is still in its infancy stage, the author proposes some set of recommendations to protect the unaccompanied migrant minors who are arriving at the shores of Italy.

Firstly, one of the problems that have been identified is the lack of adequacy between the international treaty and the Italian law on the right of an unaccompanied migrant minor to have access to a legal guardian. There are gaps between the procedure and stages in addressing the specific needs of unaccompanied migrant minors. The effect of these inadequacies is that the child is suffering from discrimination. This has often resulted in the denial of being integrated into society, getting appropriate legal status, and entering the health care and education system. It is, therefore, suggested that there is a need to develop best practices, operational manual and Standard Operating Procedures (SOPs) for all processes specified in the provision of the Zampa Law, such as the appointment of well-functioned legal guardianship system and also have a harmonised European system and development of national policies and standards to measure up with the Convention on the Right of the Child against international best practices.

Secondly, as provided by the international principles in the appointment, roles and responsibilities of a guardian, the major success factor is for the guardian to work in the best interest of unaccompanied migrant minors, as the instruments require that an unaccompanied child must be accorded a guardian or a representative and that there should be a well-established framework that will consider and act in the best interest of the child. One of the qualities of a guardian, as provided by these international instruments, is that they must have the required expertise and be in charge of the child's wellness, safety, vulnerability, and development. It is discovered that the Italian National Child Protection System lacks the required guardianship system as provided under international law. Therefore, the author recommends that there should be an updated uniform guardianship framework that is in line with the rules and regulations of international law. There should also be independent national guardianship experts to spearhead Italy's local voluntary guardianship system. Another major hindrance to volunteer guardianship for unaccompanied minors is the lack of funds to carry out these huge responsibilities. The author recommends the establishment of special funds and resources for the smooth running of the guardianship system, and there should be a provision of an awareness campaign to the public on the demanding roles and responsibilities of voluntary guardianship and the benefits attached.

Additionally, to complement the role of the guardianship system for unaccompanied migrant minors arriving in Italy, the Italian government should establish good professional guardianship institutes that will help in the training and certifications of both institutional guardians and certified register of voluntary guardians and as well organise workshops and seminars to update the guardians on new measures. The Institute will also train and collaborate with the local NGOs, including judicial authorities and the municipality, to impart knowledge, skills and techniques to the voluntary guardians who serve the unaccompanied minors better. This will also include establishing a specialised judicial system to appoint guardians for unaccompanied migrant children.

Finally, the immigration officers should be trained on the practicality of the new Italian Zampa Law. It is also suggested that immigration officers or units undergo training once a year from experts trained in the field of children. The training will enhance their capacities and capabilities in providing an adequate and integrated response to unaccompanied migrant minors.

The major key stakeholders have both direct and indirect impacts on the effectiveness of having a legal guardian for unaccompanied migrant minors in Italy in line with Goals 5, 10 and 16 of the SDGs, which focus on gender equality and empowering women and girls, reduced inequality within and among countries, and promotion of peace and justice and build strong institutions. The table below summarises the stakeholders' roles and their positive influence on unaccompanied migrant minors.

Table 1: Stakeholders on effective guardianship system for unaccompanied migrant minors

SN	Stakeholder	Role
1.	The Italian Government	o Facilitate the implementation of the Zampa Law for the effectiveness of the guardianship system of unaccompanied migrant minors in its systems. o Enforce laws on the proposed project for effective guardianship systems. o Amend the existing civil and criminal laws on the proposed guardianship systems for unaccompanied migrant minors, which may assist in good governance.
2.	Immigration Officers	Take cognisance of the Zampa Law in all their various responsibilities and duties related to unaccompanied migrant minors.
3.	Human rights activists and bar associations	o Encourage the use of effective guardianship. o Make judicial opinion on promoting effective guardianship to protect unaccompanied migrant minors.
4.	NGOs, CSOs and Religious Institutions	o Enhance knowledge of law students by teaching and encouraging the use of guardianship. o Promote guardianship through research, meetings, seminars, conferences, and religious gatherings.

5.	Judiciary System	Take cognisance of guardianship when making decisions related to unaccompanied migrant minors.
6.	Media Coverage	o Raise public awareness of the effectiveness of guardianship in the Italian community. o Educate the public through articles and TV and Radio programs on how effective guardianship can be a good solution in protecting unaccompanied migrant minors.
7.	Law Researchers and Students	Write comparative papers, articles and journals on the effectiveness of guardianship to migrant minors in Italy.
8.	Adolescents Minors	To model themselves as responsible migrant minor to the effectiveness of the guardianship.
9.	UNPF	To assist in the campaigning of the implementation of the Zampa Law within the UN System and African Union.

ABOUT THE AUTHOR

Elizabeth Bose Olorunda Bien-Aime is an LL.M. holder in Rule of Law and Development from Loyola University Law School, Chicago, United States of America. She enjoys advocating for children, outings, and reading. She also holds an LL.B and Post-Graduate Diploma in Public International Law from the University of London, United Kingdom. She is a Member of the University of London Alumni, Loyola University Chicago Alumni, Loyola University Chicago School of Law Alumni and PROLAW Alumni Network. She has worked with the African Union Commission and the United Nations Economic Commission for Africa. She is a Member of the project Matrix of the Ambassadors and Heads of Mission Spouses and Diplomatic Spouses Group (AHMSDSG) and the United Nations Spouses Group in Ethiopia.

Elizabeth's writing centres on laws concerning children and the youth. She is a mentor, coach, and advocate for children, women, and the underprivileged.

BIBLIOGRAPHY

44/25, General Assembly resolution. n.d. *united nations.* http://www.ohchr.org/EN/ProfessionalInterest/Pages/CRC.aspx.

AIDA Database. 2022. *Country Report: Legal representation of unaccompanied children.* 20 May. Accessed January 31, 2023. https://asylumineurope.org/reports/country/italy/asylum-procedure/guarantees-vulnerable-groups/legal-representation-unaccompanied-children/#:~:text=The%20Reception%20Decree%20provides%20that%20the%20unaccompanied%20child,evaluation%20of%20the%20situation%.

n.d. *Alonso, N. 2016. Europe is failing refugee and migrant children, Oxfam. Available online at https://www.oxfamamerica.org/press/europe-is-failing-refugee-and-migrant-children/. Accessed on 13/02/2018.* .

Butler, Israel. 2013. *The EU Charter of Fundamental Rights: What Can It Do?* Feb. https://www.opensocietyfoundations.org/briefing-papers/eu-charter-fundamental-rights-what-can-it-do.

COMMITTEE ON THE RIGHTS OF THE CHILD. 2005. *Treatment of unaccompanied and separated children.* 17 - 3 May - June. Accessed January 31, 2023. http://www2.ohchr.org/english/bodies/crc/docs/GC6.pdf.

Constitution, Italian. n.d. *Chapter 117.* https://www.senato.it/documenti/repository/istituzione/costituzione_inglese.pdf.

Council of Europe. 1996. "European Convention on the Exercise of Children's Rights." *European Treaty Series - No. 160.* Strasbourg, 25 January. Accessed January 27, 2023. https://rm.coe.int/european-convention-on-the-exercise-of-children-s-rights/1680a40f72.

Davies, Gareth. 2017. *Mail online.* 11 may. https://www.dailymail.co.uk/news/article-4496094/63-000-migrants-came-EU-unaccompanied-minors-2016.html.

Defense for Children International Italia OdV . n.d. *THE GLOBAL MOVEMENT FOR CHILDREN'S AND YOUTH'S RIGHTS.* Accessed January 30, 2023. https://www.defenceforchildren.it/it/news-34/documenti-utili.

European Union. 2000. "Charter of Fundamental Rights." *Official Journal of the European Communities* (European Union) 20-24. Accessed January 27, 2023. https://www.europarl.europa.eu/charter/pdf/text_en.pdf.

French Documentation. 2013. *Italy: a European destiny.* La Documentation française. https://www.vie-publique.fr/catalogue/23292-litalie-un-destin-europeen.

1990. *International Convention on the Protection of the Rights of All Migrant Workers and Members of Their Families.* 18 december. https://www.ohchr.org/en/instruments-mechanisms/instruments/international-convention-protection-rights-all-migrant-workers.

International Maritime Organization (IMO). 1979. *International Convention on Maritime Search and Rescue.* London. Accessed January 27, 2023. https://www.imo.org/en/About/Conventions/Pages/International-Convention-on-Maritime-Search-and-Rescue-(SAR).aspx.

International Organisation for Migration (IOM). n.d. *About Migration.* Accessed January 26, 2023. https://www.iom.int/about-migration.

Ministry of Labor and Social Policies - Directorate for

Immigration and Integration Policies. 2020. *Italy: Report on unaccompanied minors.* Government Report, European Commission. Accessed January 25, 2023. https://ec.europa.eu/migrant-integration/library-document/italy-report-unaccompanied-minors_en.

Minorisna. 2017. *New Italian law to protect unaccompanied refugee and migrant children.* 13 April. Accessed January 30, 2023. https://medium.com/@minorisna/new-italian-law-to-protect-unaccompanied-refugee-and-migrantchildren-3670a68b59d4.

2019. *Office Of Refugee Resettlement* . 18 March. https://www.acf.hhs.gov/orr/uac-infographic.

Office of the Refugee Applications Commissioner (ORAC). 2013. *EU Dublin III Regulation (Regulation (EU) No 604/2013).* Accessed January 27, 2023. http://www.orac.ie/website/orac/oracwebsite.nsf/page/eudublinIIIregulation-main-en#.

Pianta, Mario. 2020. "The Rise of Populism: Case Studies, Determinants and Policy Implications." *Italy's Political Upheaval and the Consequences of Inequality*, 13–17.

n.d. *Rapporto Nationle.* http://www.defenceforchildren.it/files/RAPPORTO_NAZIONALE_SG.pdf .

2014. *REGULATION (EU) No 516/2014 OF THE EUROPEAN PARLIAMENT AND OF THE COUNCIL.* THE EUROPEAN PARLIAMENT AND THE COUNCIL OF THE EUROPEAN UNION.

2018. *Reliefweb.* 30 May. https://reliefweb.int/report/italy/italy-more-100-unaccompanied-foreign-minors-helped-first-quarter-i-care-about-you.

UK Goverment Home Office. 2020. *Dublin III Regulation.* London, 2020 August. Accessed January 27, 2023. https://assets.publishing.service.gov.uk/government/uploads/system/uploads/attachment_data/file/909412/

dublin-III-regulation.pdf.

UN Department of Economic and Social Affairs. 2015. *Sustainable Development.* Accessed January 27, 2023. https://sdgs.un.org/goals.

UN General Assembly. 2017. *Resolution adopted by the Human Rights Council on 28 September 2017.* 6 October. https://docstore.ohchr.org/SelfServices/FilesHandler.ashx?enc=dtYoAzPhJ4NMy4Lu1TOebIM8c1X4G-ZjGEGHV9SBM9XQ6I3RcfsWkCIHIU3MdP8C-qRC51wZQTdxYCQRWsQG5JDHTVdkE9qC%2FA9Uy-tOdHTprv7VCn9w06t5AfOm3vSlivt.

UNICEF. 2019. *More than 6,100 unaccompanied refugee and migrant children in Italy in need of community and family-based care.* 5 dec. https://www.unicef.org/press-releases/more-6100-unaccompanied-refugee-and-migrant-children-italy-need-community-and-family.

United Nations High Commissioner for Refugees. 2017. *UNHCR Europe Monthly Report.* 31 October. Accessed February 01, 2023. https://reliefweb.int/report/italy/unhcr-europe-monthly-report-october-2017.

United Nations. n.d. *Universal Declaration of Human Rights.* Accessed January 27, 2023. http://www.un.org/en/universal-declaration-human-rights/index.html.

Zandonini, Giacomo. 2017. *The long wait of young unaccompanied migrants in Italy.* 8 February. Accessed January 30, 2023. https://openmigration.org/en/analyses/the-long-wait-of-young-unaccompanied-migrants-in-italy/.

www.ingramcontent.com/pod-product-compliance
Lightning Source LLC
LaVergne TN
LVHW100329210926
848480LV00003B/1294